Just Stay Calm

How to Think Clearly and Make Safe Decisions in a Digital World

Donald
Tate

Just Stay Calm Publishing
Florida

Just Stay Calm

Published by:
Just Stay Calm Publishing
https://www.juststaycalm.com

Author:
Donald Tate

Paperback ISBN: 979-8-9964233-1-6
Hardcover ISBN: 979-8-9964233-0-9

First Edition

Printed in the United States of America

"Technology is everywhere. Guidance is not."
— Donald Tate

"For fast-acting relief, try slowing down."
— Jane Wagner

For my wife, my family, and everyone who believed I could help others navigate the world a little more calmly.

Pull Up a Chair

Hey there. Grab a chair and have a seat.

Before we begin, I wanted you to know something important.

You do not need to be or become a technology expert to navigate the digital world safely. You also don't have to be afraid to be safe.

You don't even need to memorize a list of scams or keep up with every new app, platform, or headline.

What you need is a calm, repeatable way to think through situations when something feels rushed, confusing, emotional, or just a little off.

That's why "Just Stay Calm" is intentionally simple. Not because the situations we will discuss are simple, but because people think more clearly when they have a simple process to follow under pressure.

Throughout this book, you may notice ideas being repeated.

That's intentional.

The goal is to help the process become familiar enough that it feels natural when you need it most.

Read the book at your own pace, whatever that is.

Some people will work through it in a day or two.

Other people may stop often to reflect, revisit sections, or discuss ideas with friends and family.

Both approaches work, and you get to decide how you want to learn this process.

There's no test, no expectation that you will remember every detail.

There is only a hope that you will finish this book with a calmer mindset, more confidence, and a clearer process for handling digital situations that feel off. And maybe just a bit more.

While reading this book, you may find yourself thinking about people in your own life: a parent, spouse, child, friend, or neighbor. Someone who needs to hear this information.

That's normal.

Many helpful conversations begin that way. One person slows down, begins to understand things differently, and then helps someone else do the same.

Over time, you may notice yourself feeling a little calmer, a little more confident, and a little less rushed when something feels off.

So, grab a cup of joe or tea, settle back in your chair, flip some pages, and take the time you need while we walk through this together.

Table of Contents

A Different Way to Think About Staying Safe

Most advice about staying safe online feels overwhelming.

Whether you read an article, someone shares a list, or you sit through a presentation, it suddenly feels like there are a hundred things you're supposed to remember.

Do this. Don't do that. Watch out for this. Avoid that. Use this tool. Install that protection. What starts as helpful quickly turns into a growing list of rules that feels less like guidance and more like pressure and a requirement to spend more money.

The more you research, the easier it becomes to believe that staying safe requires being perfect.

That is where most people quietly start stepping back. Not because they don't care or are careless, but because it starts to feel like it is too much.

You don't sit down at your computer thinking, "Today is the day I will use everything I know about online safety."

You are busy answering messages, checking emails, paying bills, looking something up, helping someone else, and generally moving through your day. Life doesn't slow down just because something might be a scam. In fact, most scams show up when life is already moving fast.

This book takes a different approach.

It's not going to give you a long list of rules to memorize or expect you to suddenly become technical and able to recognize every scam.

That's not how people stay safe.

People stay safe because of how they respond in the moments when something feels off.

When you study situations in which people are taken advantage of, the issue is not a lack of knowledge. It's not that they didn't know enough, or that they made a careless decision on purpose.

It is that something happened quickly, and they reacted before they had time to think.

That moment between awareness and decision is where everything changes, and it is the moment this book focuses on. Because if you can change what happens at that moment, you can change the outcome.

Everything in this book is built around a single idea, that's simple enough to remember even when everything else feels uncertain: "Just Stay Calm."

It may not sound like much right now, and it may even feel too simple. But when you consider the moments when people get caught off guard, it becomes clear why it matters.

Scammers don't rely on weak security protocols or complex tricks as much as people might think. They rely on urgency, pressure, and emotion to get you to act before you have time to see what's really happening.

They're not trying to outsmart you with a long, complicated scheme. They're trying to make you speed up.

When you feel rushed, you don't always stop to evaluate, verify, or question what you are seeing the way you would if you had a little more time. Instead, you just respond, and once you respond, the rest becomes easier for them.

That's why calm matters.

Staying calm does not mean you ignore things. It does not mean you avoid problems or pretend something is not happening. It means giving yourself a moment to think before you act. Even a few seconds can change everything.

That moment allows you to step back, instead of stepping in.

It gives you space to notice things that otherwise would be missed, and it puts you back in control of the situation instead of letting it control you.

That is what we are building here. Not a system that requires perfection, but a way of responding that works in real life, even when you are busy, distracted, or dealing with something important.

This book isn't something you need to memorize. It is something you become familiar with.

The way it is structured is intentional. The table of contents is not just organizing chapters; it will help you find your place when you need it most.

If something happens and you are unsure what to do, you can open this book, find the section that matches your current moment, and read it at your own pace.

There's no pressure to get it perfect, and no expectation that you'll never make a mistake. This is about building awareness and confidence.

As you progress through this book, you will start noticing patterns. Not complicated or technical patterns, but simple signals that show up repeatedly in different forms, like messages that feel rushed, requests that seem familiar but aren't quite right, situations that feel just a little too good to be true.

When a situation occurs, you may not be able to explain exactly why something feels off, and that's okay. This is just your first signal that something deserves a closer look.

Once you begin noticing these patterns, your responses start to change. You pause, think, and take a moment before acting. That pause becomes your advantage. Instead of reacting, you begin to respond intentionally. Instead of feeling uncertain, you feel more in control.

That is the shift this book is designed to create.

Not perfection. Not technical expertise. Just a simple, repeatable way to stay in control when something does not feel right.

The truth is you already have most of what you need. You already know how to question things and recognize when something does not feel quite right. The only thing you need is a way to slow down enough to use that instinct when it matters most.

This book will help you do that step by step, moment by moment, in a way that fits into real life.

And it all starts with something simple enough to remember when everything else feels uncertain:

Just stay calm.

Why This Happens

Most people believe that scams happen to people who are not paying attention, are not careful, or do not understand technology. That belief feels comforting because it creates distance. It allows us to think, "That would not happen to me." But that is not how it works.

Scams are not built around who you are. They're built around where and when you are. They happen in moments shaped by pressure, timing, and emotion.

They're built around numbers, not names. No one is sitting somewhere choosing you specifically.

These systems are designed to reach thousands of people at a time, waiting for the right moment to connect with someone who is distracted, stressed, or simply trying to do the right thing.

When that moment happens, everything feels different. It doesn't feel like a scam. It feels like something that needs to be handled.

That's where one loving wife's story begins.

She wasn't thinking about scams. She was thinking about her husband. He was nearing the end of his life, a veteran who had spent years taking care of others, and now she was trying to take care of him at home.

The doctors had been clear: if she wanted to keep him comfortable, she would need certain equipment. This equipment wasn't optional; it was essential for his daily care.

So, she did what anyone would do. She went online and searched carefully for the equipment. She looked for something that felt right, something safe, something that made sense for a veteran on a fixed income. She was not rushing; she was trying to do the right thing. And then she found a site that seemed to understand exactly what she needed.

The site looked legitimate, the language felt right, and it spoke directly to her needs in a way that felt trustworthy. When something feels like it understands your situation, you don't approach it with suspicion; you approach it with relief.

So, she didn't hesitate. She placed the order to get the equipment sooner. At that moment, there was no reason to pause. She had found what was needed and acted. She was moving forward.

Then she waited.

At first, nothing seemed wrong. Delays happen, especially with medical equipment. Days passed, then more days. Eventually, the lack of delivery became hard to ignore, but even then, it didn't immediately feel like a scam. It felt like something that had not gone as planned. Then, slowly, a different thought began to form; something was not right.

That moment of discovery is quiet. It doesn't come with alarms or warnings. It arrives as a simple feeling, one you're not ready to accept. And when it does, it often brings something else with it: silence.

She didn't tell anyone not because she couldn't, but because saying it out loud would make it real. And once it was real, it would carry weight. It would raise questions. It would invite judgment, even if that judgment never actually came. So instead, she kept the situation to herself.

She tried to move forward, to adjust, to figure things out quietly. Weeks passed, and life continued, but the problem remained unresolved.

Then an email arrived. It offered exactly what she had been looking for: the same type of equipment, the same kind of support, the same sense that someone understood her needs. It did not feel random; it felt timely.

If you pause and imagine that moment, already dealing with something difficult, already trying to solve a real problem, and suddenly something appears that seems to help, you can understand why it would not immediately raise suspicion.

It felt like a second chance, so she tried again. But this attempt ended the same way as the first.

What she did not know was that it was the same group behind it, the same pattern, the same approach, just delivered differently. From her perspective, it did not feel like repetition. It felt like another attempt to do the right thing. When it failed again, the weight of that realization became harder to bear.

At some point, she made the difficult decision to tell her son. Not because everything was clear, and not because she suddenly understood what had happened, but because she decided she did not have to handle it alone anymore. That single decision changed everything.

Together, they began to look at what had happened, not in panic, but with patience. They walked through the process to understand what could have been affected. They secured her accounts, verified her finances, and resumed searching for the right equipment. Eventually, they found a legitimate source for the equipment she needed, and the greatest part of the problem was solved.

The real value in this story is not in how it was resolved. It is in understanding why it happened in the first place. Nothing she did was overtly careless. Nothing she did was unreasonable. In fact, nothing she did was different from what others do every day.

She was trying to take care of someone she loved. She was under pressure. She found something that felt right, and when something went wrong, she tried to correct it. Every part of that is normal.

That is the part that matters.

When you look at situations like this from the outside, it is easy to focus on the outcome. It is easy to say what should have been done differently.

But inside the moment, it feels very different. Different situation. Different person. Same pattern. Something appears at the right time. It feels real. It feels helpful. It feels like the right thing to do. And in that moment, action comes before reflection.

That is what we are going to change. Not by memorizing rules. Not by trying to recognize every scam. But by learning to recognize the patterns that show up repeatedly, no matter what form they take.

Once you begin to see those patterns, something shifts. You begin to pause and ask questions. You begin to take back control of the moment. And that is where everything starts to change.

Rushing Hurts

There's a moment in most situations when people later realize something went wrong, and it's not the moment most people think it is.

It's not when money is sent, information is shared, or a decision is made. Those are outcomes. The moment that matters happens earlier and often goes unnoticed.

It begins when something unexpectedly captures your attention.

A message appears, a notification interrupts, a call comes through, or an event presents itself that feels important enough to take priority over whatever you were doing.

This causes a subtle shift in focus, and without realizing it, you begin moving toward solving whatever has just been placed in front of you. This shift doesn't feel dangerous. It feels responsible.

In everyday life, responding quickly is often the right thing to do.

We are conditioned to answer messages, return calls, and handle tasks as they come in. That behavior is normal and constantly reinforced. The problem is not the instinct to respond. The problem is what happens when that instinct is used against you.

In those moments, something else enters and changes the way you think. It may not be obvious at first, but it's there. It can take the form of urgency, pressure, or even opportunity.

It creates a feeling that something needs to be handled now, not later. While that feeling is present, you don't think in your normal patterns.

Normally, you'd evaluate information before acting. You'd consider what you're seeing, compare it to what you know, and take time to decide what to do next. You might even pause, step away, or ask someone else for input.

That process happens naturally when there is no pressure. Under pressure, the process speeds up and constricts.

You begin to react faster, read more quickly, and make decisions in haste.

It doesn't feel like you're skipping steps. It feels like you're handling something that truly needs attention. That is the moment where control starts to shift.

The situation itself has not changed. The information in front of you is the same as it would be if you were calm. What has changed is the speed at which you are processing it.

That change reduces the space between seeing something and acting on it, and that's the space where good decisions are made.

When that space is reduced, small details become easier to miss.

A message that might have felt unusual earlier now feels acceptable. A request that might have raised questions now feels fine. The context that would normally guide your thinking becomes secondary to the need to respond.

This is often just a human response to pressure.

If you look outside of technology, the same pattern exists. When something seems urgent, people respond differently. They move faster, prioritize the immediate issue, and focus on resolving it quickly.

That behavior is useful in many situations, which is why it is so deeply ingrained in all of us.

The difference in these situations is that the urgency isn't always real. It's created and introduced in a way that feels natural, but its purpose is to move you away from your normal decision-making process and push you toward action before you fully understand what is happening.

Once you begin to recognize this urgency, you start to see it appear in things like emails suggesting something will expire soon, messages about a problem that needs to be fixed immediately, or opportunities with cash value but a time limit. On the surface, each looks different, but they share the same structure: they create a need for speed that changes how you think.

And that change is what matters.

If you're not aware, the process continues automatically. You see something, feel the pressure, and respond. By the time you slow down and reflect, the decision has already been made.

If you are aware of it, something different happens.

You notice the feeling itself, the sense that something is pushing you to move faster than you normally would. That awareness creates a small amount of space, even if only a few seconds.

In that space, you have a choice. You can continue moving at the same pace or slow down.

Slowing down does not mean ignoring the situation. It means choosing to return to the way you think when you're not under pressure or emotion. That choice changes everything.

It allows you to reintroduce the steps that were being shortened. You begin to evaluate, question, and consider whether the urgency is real.

This is not about memorizing scenarios. It is about recognizing when your thinking is being influenced by pressure.

That recognition does not require technical knowledge. It only requires awareness of a feeling most people have experienced many times: the feeling that something needs to happen right now.

Once you can identify that feeling and separate it from the situation, you begin to see that urgency is not always tied to reality, and the sense of urgency loses some of its power. It does not disappear, but it no longer controls the moment in the same way.

This is where staying calm becomes a deliberate response to a specific moment. When you recognize that your thinking is being rushed, staying calm becomes the action that creates space. That space allows you to move from reacting to responding, and that shift is what changes outcomes.

This shift shows you that situations themselves are not as unique as they first appear. They may look different, but the way they influence your thinking follows a consistent pattern.

A message may suggest something will expire soon. A call may introduce a problem that needs immediate attention, or an opportunity may feel limited. Each creates the same effect: it compresses your decision-making process.

When time feels limited, you focus on the immediate task instead of the full context. You move toward the first solution that seems to work. That is not a flaw. It's a natural response. Recognizing it allows you to step back and breathe.

Instead of solving the situation immediately, you shift your focus to the process. You ask whether you are being pushed to move too fast, or if this speed fits the situation.

At this point, small questions become powerful:

Why does this need to happen now?

What changes if I wait?

Is there another way to confirm this?

These questions interrupt the automatic process and create space. In many cases, that's enough because when urgency isn't real, it doesn't hold up under scrutiny.

Even when a suspected issue turns out to be a real need, slowing down doesn't create a problem. Real issues do not require immediate action without verification. And real opportunities do not disappear the moment you ask a question.

Once you begin to recognize that, urgency starts to feel different. It becomes something to examine, not simply follow.

You are no longer reacting. You are deciding how to engage. You create space to recognize when something does not feel right or line up the way it should.

That space is created by intentionally staying calm.

That calm comes from the decision not to match the speed of whatever is pushing you. From that point, everything else becomes easier. You evaluate more clearly, verify more effectively, and disengage when necessary.

This chapter isn't introducing something new. It helps you recognize something that already exists: the moment when thinking changes under pressure.

Once you can see that moment, you can control it.

And once you can control it, you can change what happens next.

Appendix B includes several examples of situations that may initially feel off, along with calm explanations of what they may represent.

Something's Off

Most events have a moment where something feels off not completely wrong, but not quite right either. Not strong enough to trigger an immediate reaction, but not clear enough to suggest a problem. The moment sits somewhere in between, which makes it easy to ignore.

The event could be a message that seems slightly unusual, a request that feels a bit out of place, or an inquiry that appears normal but carries a small sense of uncertainty. No matter the type of event, these moments are often dismissed because they lack sufficient evidence and are easy to explain away, especially when everything else appears to be okay.

Negative situations rarely begin with something obvious. If they did, they would be easy to avoid. Instead, they begin with something that feels familiar, something that fits within your expectations of how things should be.

That familiarity creates a sense of comfort, lowering your guard.

It's important to note that familiarity is not the actual problem. It is something people rely on every day to navigate events quickly and efficiently. We recognize patterns, environments, and behaviors that allow us to move through our day without analyzing every detail, and that is a necessary part of functioning in a busy world.

The problem begins when familiarity influences your decisions without you realizing it.

When something feels familiar, it often feels safe, and you're more likely to accept it as part of your normal experience, even if there are minor inconsistencies. Those inconsistencies are where the signal exists, but they're easy to miss because they are surrounded by things that appear correct.

When you think about environments designed to feel safe, widely used platforms, systems with protection in place, and accounts configured correctly. All these elements contribute to a sense of security. They create the impression that risks have already been addressed and that the environment itself can be trusted.

That trust is often justified, but it can also create blind spots.

Let's consider an event that was shared with me, involving a young child who was starting to use online games with chat features. The gaming account had been set up properly, parental controls were in place, and the environment appeared safe. From the outside, everything looked correct, and there was no immediate reason for concern.

However, while using the in-game chat, a conversation began that seemed no different than others the child had experienced. It followed the same patterns as many other conversations within that environment, and because of that, it felt normal.

Over time, the conversation shifted. The other user introduced the idea of improving progress in the game quickly, presenting it as something to make the game better. It didn't feel like a demand; it felt like an opportunity. There was one additional detail, though: the opportunity was limited.

They could only help the child for a very short period. Waiting would mean losing the chance; acting quickly would secure the benefit.

At that point, the situation was familiar, helpful, and urgent.

Each element alone might not create a problem, but together they begin to shape how the situation is understood. Add the fact that the child was untrained in using online chat and games, and you have a real opportunity for a negative outcome.

Eventually, the child became rushed and responded quickly to what felt like a reasonable opportunity. There was no feeling that anything wrong was being suggested. The goal was simply to improve gameplay through a known shortcut.

However, to receive this help, the other user needed money that the child didn't have. That's when the other user suggested using a parent's credit card, claiming the parents could dispute the charge later and get their money back. This was something the other user claimed to do all the time, and they never got in trouble.

After some nervous moments of pressure to hurry up, the child agreed to pay without the same level of questioning that might occur in non-pressured situations. They knew where a credit card was, and they had been convinced the parents would approve if asked. After all, the other user pointed out, the child had been doing well in school, and this was just a small reward.

The environment felt safe, the interaction seemed normal, and the urgency created a sense that action should be taken quickly.

By this point, the decision process had already been manipulated, and the child gave the credit card information to the other user.

As luck would have it, the transaction was blocked because the parents had locked the card as a safety precaution. This prevented an immediate loss of money.

From a technical standpoint, protection was in place, and it prevented an immediate outcome.

But an important part of the situation has already occurred. The decision had been made, and the attempt to act had already happened. What prevented a loss was not the child's decision-making, but external control.

That distinction matters because it highlights the difference between protection and awareness. The system provided one layer of protection by blocking the transaction, and that's valuable. It prevented an immediate loss, but it did not address the underlying issue of how the situation was interpreted and how the decision was made.

That part remained unchanged.

While reviewing the situation later, it became clear that nothing in the environment had been obviously wrong. The child's account was set up correctly, the platform was widely used, and the interaction followed familiar patterns.

What was missing was an understanding of how to evaluate what was happening within that environment.

No one had explained what to watch for. No one had described how these interactions could influence decisions. No one had connected the idea that something could feel normal and still require attention. But mostly, no one had thought that the environment could not fully protect against this, even with its safety features in place.

This is where awareness becomes critical.

When something feels off, it doesn't always present itself clearly. There may not be enough information to recognize it as a problem, but it often includes subtle signals indicating a closer look is needed. Learning to recognize those signals changes how you respond.

Instead of dismissing the feeling because everything appears correct, you begin to treat it as a reason to pause. You do not need to identify exactly what's wrong; you only need to acknowledge that something doesn't fully align with expectations.

That acknowledgment creates space to evaluate the situation more carefully.

You can now consider whether the interaction makes sense, whether the request is appropriate, and whether the urgency is justified. These actions don't require advanced knowledge; they require a willingness to slow down and question what's happening, even when it feels familiar.

That is the shift.

It's not about avoiding every risk. It's about recognizing when something deserves your attention, even if it does not appear to be a problem at first glance.

Once you develop that awareness, the feeling that something is "off" becomes useful. It becomes a signal you can't ignore, leading to better decisions. Situations that would previously have gone unnoticed start to stand out in small but meaningful ways.

Instead of focusing on what is being presented, you notice how it feels. That may seem subtle, but it has a powerful impact on how you process information. It allows you to detect inconsistencies that may not be immediately visible on the surface.

This is where three common patterns begin to appear more clearly: urgency, familiarity, and value.

Urgency creates pressure to act quickly, reducing the space available for evaluation.

Familiarity creates comfort, making an event feel normal even when elements do not fully align.

Value encourages focus on what you can gain, at the expense of noticing what you might be missing.

Each of these patterns can exist on their own, but they are most effective when combined.

When something feels familiar, offers value, and creates urgency, it becomes much harder to evaluate objectively. The situation feels normal, beneficial, and time-sensitive all at once, encouraging action without reflection.

When you encounter a situation that includes one or more of these patterns, the goal should not be to assume something is wrong. The goal should be to slow down and examine the situation more carefully.

This is where staying calm becomes practical.

When something feels off, staying calm gives you the space to evaluate. Without that space, the patterns continue to influence your thinking. With it, you can begin to ask simple questions:

Does this need to happen right now?

Does this make sense in the context of what I know?

Is there another way to confirm this?

These questions are not meant to provide immediate answers.

They are meant to interrupt the automatic process that occurs when familiarity, urgency, and value are present. That interruption is often enough to reveal inconsistencies in what you're being asked to respond to.

Even when the event turns out to be legitimate, this process does no harm. Taking time to evaluate does not prevent real opportunities or delay real solutions. It simply ensures your response is based on a clearer understanding of what is happening.

You are not trying to avoid interactions. You're trying to improve how you engage with them.

That improvement comes from recognizing the signals that something deserves more attention. Over time, this becomes easier. What once felt like a vague sense of uncertainty begins to take shape. You start recognizing patterns more quickly, and your responses become more consistent.

That consistency is what creates control.

It allows you to move through events with confidence, not because you know everything, but because you have a reliable way of responding when something doesn't feel right.

When something feels off, that is your signal to pause, not to assume, but to evaluate; not to follow pressure, but to understand it.

That shift allows you to move forward with clarity. And that clarity is what prevents problems from developing further.

Just Stay Calm

Up to this point, everything we've discussed has been building toward a single idea. Not a complex system, not a technical solution, but a simple way to respond when something doesn't feel right: Just Stay Calm.

This can sound almost too simple at first. In a world where problems often seem complicated, the expectation is that solutions must be equally complex. That assumption is part of what makes this approach different.

Staying calm is not about ignoring what's happening or pretending nothing is happening. It's not about delaying action or avoiding responsibility. It's about choosing how you respond in the moment. Your instinct is to move quickly, and that choice becomes the foundation for everything that follows.

When you think back to the situation in Chapter 2, when the wife tried to buy medical equipment for her husband, a pattern begins to emerge. There is a moment when something captures your attention, a moment when urgency or familiarity begins to influence thinking, and a moment when a decision is made.

That sequence happens quickly, and without a way to interrupt it, the outcome is often determined before there's time to understand what's happening.

Staying calm is not just helpful here; it's essential.

It creates a pause, and that pause marks the point where the process changes. Instead of moving directly from recognizing a situation to acting on it, staying calm introduces a step in between. It allows you to slow down just enough to regain control of how you normally think.

And that is where the method begins.

Not as a specific list of instructions, but a way to move through events in a controlled, consistent manner. The goal isn't to memorize steps. The goal is to create a flow that becomes natural over time, a way of responding you can rely on.

So, remember, when something feels off, you do not need to define what is wrong. You don't need to decide whether it is legitimate. Those answers come later. First, you need to create space. Space to think, space to evaluate, and space to decide how to proceed.

Staying calm creates that space. Once it exists, you can begin to move through the situation deliberately. You are no longer reacting to what's in front of you; you are engaging with it, and that distinction is important. Reacting is fast and automatic, following the path presented. Engagement is slower and intentional, allowing you to choose your path instead of following one designed for you.

The "Just Stay Calm" method is designed to support that engagement. It provides a structure you can follow without needing to think about every detail in the moment. Over time, it becomes something you rely on naturally, without consciously recalling each part. That is what makes it effective. It is simple enough for real situations but structured enough to guide your decisions.

The process begins with recognizing something feels off, not necessarily because you can't explain it, but because it doesn't align with your expectations. Recognition then leads to a pause, which creates space. In that space, you begin to look at the situation differently. Not trying to solve it immediately but trying to understand it.

From there, you begin to evaluate what you are seeing, comparing it to what you already know.

You look for details that either support or contradict what is being presented, and if something does not align, you move to verify it.

Verifying is not about confirming what you hope is true. It is about confirming what is true by using sources outside the immediate situation.

If something still feels off at this point, you create distance. You step back, disengage, and remove yourself from the immediate interaction to maintain or regain control of the process.

From there, you decide if any action needs to be taken to protect yourself or your information. You review what has happened not with urgency, but with clarity. If necessary, you can involve others by reporting the situation or sharing it with someone who can provide additional perspective or assistance.

Finally, you carry that experience forward. You share what you've learned with others not as a warning rooted in fear, but in a way that builds awareness and confidence.

That's the flow.

Each part connects to the next to support the overall goal of staying in control. It's not about perfection. It's about consistency. When you follow this process, you stop making decisions under pressure or with incomplete information.

You create a system that works across all situations, regardless of how they are presented. This is what makes the method reliable.

It doesn't depend on identifying specific scenarios. It depends on how you respond to the patterns that appear within the moments you are involved in, regardless of what the presented information looks like.

By focusing on your response instead of the situation itself, you create a level of control that is not easily disrupted. That control begins with a simple decision to just stay calm. Not a passive reaction, but an active choice that allows everything else in the process to work. Without that choice, the method doesn't begin. With it, all the steps become possible.

It's worth noting that when a process is simple, it's easy to underestimate its value. There's a tendency to believe that something must be complex to be effective, especially when addressing events that feel complicated or unpredictable. This method is intentionally simple. Not because events that come our way are simple, but because simplicity naturally counters complexity.

Simplicity is what allows this process to work, not in theory, but in real-world situations. When something feels urgent or unfamiliar, you don't have time to recall detailed instructions or analyze every possibility. You need something that fits into the moment without adding to the pressure.

Each part connects to the next in a way that mirrors how events unfold. You're not jumping between unrelated steps. You are moving through a sequence that aligns with how you naturally process information when not under pressure. Following that sequence, even under pressure, creates a more consistent response.

Consistency is what turns a process into something you can rely on.

Without it, every situation feels new, and you're forced to figure out what to do from the beginning every time. With it, you have a familiar path to follow, even when situations feel off.

This is where repetition becomes valuable.

As you move through this process over time, the steps begin to reinforce each other. You begin to recognize where you are in the flow without having to think about it. The transition from one part to the next becomes more natural, and the entire process requires less effort.

Each part of the method plays a specific role, but the parts are designed to work together as a connected system rather than isolated steps:

The initial pause creates space.

Evaluation helps you understand what you are seeing.

Verification confirms whether it is accurate.

Disengaging protects you from immediate pressure.

Protection ensures that any potential impact is addressed.

Reporting allows others to be aware of the situation.

Sharing extends that awareness beyond the immediate experience.

This process doesn't require perfect execution. Even if you move through only part of it, you are still improving your response. The key is that you are no longer moving directly from recognition to action without any interruption.

You are introducing steps that allow you to think, and that is what changes outcomes.

Without a process, your response to each situation is determined by whatever feels most immediate at the time. That response may be influenced by urgency, familiarity, or perceived value, but it is inconsistent, and that inconsistency creates risk.

With a process, your response is guided by something stable. It doesn't eliminate uncertainty, but it reduces the likelihood of making decisions based on incomplete or misleading information.

This method doesn't require special tools, advanced knowledge, or significant time. It requires awareness, consistency, and the ability to pause when something feels off.

These requirements are realistic. This is something you can apply immediately, without additional preparation, which makes it a valuable tool in your safety toolbox.

As you begin to apply this process, you may find that you feel a natural pull toward some parts more than others. That's expected. Everyone approaches situations differently, and certain steps will align more closely with how you already think.

The important part is not how quickly you adopt the entire process. It's that you begin to use it, because even small changes in how you respond can have a significant impact.

Pausing for a moment, rather than reacting immediately, can prevent a decision made under pressure.

Asking a single question can reveal information that wasn't initially considered.

Choosing to verify can prevent situations from progressing further.

These are small actions, but they are powerful. They change the flow of situations, and once that occurs, the rest of the process becomes easier to follow.

That is how the method works in practice. Nothing complex. Nothing earth-shattering.

It doesn't require you to be perfect. It requires consistency. Consistency creates familiarity with the process. Familiarity makes it easier to use, and ease of use ensures it becomes part of how you respond, rather than something you must remember to apply.

This is where the method becomes more than a set of ideas.

It becomes a habit followed all the time. A way of thinking carried into every situation. A response mechanism that supports better outcomes.

Not just a set of steps, but a reliable approach to handling anything.

And it all begins with the same simple action: just staying calm long enough to let the process work.

Pause, Breathe

If everything in this book were reduced to a single thought or action, it would be this: Just Stay Calm.

Not as a suggestion, and not as something that sounds good in theory, but as a deliberate decision you make in a specific moment.

The moment when something interrupts your day and demands attention, or when something feels urgent, important, or just slightly off, that is where this first step lives.

It's easy to underestimate how much influence a single moment can have over what happens next. By the time most people realize something may have gone wrong, several decisions have already been made quickly, and without the level of thoughtfulness they would normally have. The reason for that is not a lack of awareness; it's a change in pace.

When something feels urgent, the pace changes, and you naturally want to move faster. You read faster, interpret faster, and decide faster. That shift in speed doesn't feel like a loss of control. It feels like efficiency, like you are handling something that needs to be handled.

In many areas of life, that response is rewarded because acting quickly can be helpful and can keep things moving.

But in these situations, speed is not to your advantage; it is to theirs.

That is why this step is about interrupting the speed at which the situation is trying to move you. And that starts with staying calm.

Staying calm does not eliminate the situation, but it does change how you experience it.

Instead of being pulled into it, you create a small space to breathe. That space is not physical; it's mental. It gives you a moment to step out of the pressure and decide how you want to respond. That is where control begins.

Thinking back to the moments in the story of the wife trying to care for her husband, or the child being tricked into using his parents' credit card. In each case, there was a common point where everything could have changed.

Not by knowing more or having better information, but by slowing down before taking the next step. That is what staying calm allows you to do. It allows you to create a pause.

A pause that does not need to be long or require stepping away for an extended period. Even a few seconds are enough to interrupt the intended flow.

During that pause, thinking returns to normal. You are no longer matching the urgency of the situation. You are beginning to process it at your own pace, and that shift is subtle but powerful.

Without the pause, the original process continues. You see something, feel pressure, and respond. By the time you reflect on what happened, a decision has already been made.

With the pause, something different is possible. You notice what is happening, and instead of being absorbed by it, you begin asking different questions:

Is the urgency real?

Does this require an immediate response?

What happens if I take a few minutes to think clearly before acting?

These are small changes, but they can lead to different outcomes.

Staying calm is not always easy in these moments. The feeling of urgency can be strong. It can feel like something important is at risk or that an opportunity will be lost if you do not act quickly. That feeling is designed to push you forward. Recognizing it is part of staying calm.

You're not trying to eliminate the feeling. You are acknowledging that it exists and choosing not to let it dictate your response. That is what makes this step active rather than passive. You are purposefully deciding to do something.

That decision does not require certainty. You do not need to know the situation is real. You only need to recognize that something is trying to influence your thinking and choose to slow down. Once you do, everything else becomes easier.

The next steps in the process rely on your ability to think clearly. They depend on having enough time to evaluate what you are seeing, verify information, and decide how to proceed. Without creating that space to breathe, the next steps become difficult to apply. Staying calm is what creates that space.

If you skip this step, the process never fully begins. You move directly from recognition to action, and you continue to be influenced by the sense of urgency that is being created.

By applying this step, even briefly, the entire process shifts. You create a moment where you regain control.

Over time, this step becomes easier. The more you recognize the feeling of urgency and decide to slow down, the more natural that response becomes. What once required conscious effort becomes automatic, and you develop a habit of pausing before deciding to act.

This is why everything begins here, not with evaluating or acting, but with the decision to stay calm long enough to think clearly. That decision creates the space needed for everything else to work. Without it, even the best process becomes difficult to apply.

As simple as the idea of staying calm sounds, it becomes even more meaningful when you consider what it replaces. Without this step, most responses are driven by momentum and emotion.

A message or alert appears, creating a sense of urgency or importance. You move forward with it because that movement feels natural and aligns with how you handle most things in daily life.

The difference is that without this first step, you are no longer moving at your own pace. The situation is setting the pace for you.

That distinction is easy to miss, especially when a situation feels legitimate. There may be no obvious signs that something is wrong. The message may look correct. The request may seem reasonable. The timing may even make sense. Everything can appear to align in a way that supports action, and that is what makes these moments powerful.

When you stay calm, you are not just slowing down. You are interrupting the momentum the situation is trying to create.

That interruption allows you to step outside the immediate flow and view the situation from a different perspective.

A perspective that allows you to see more clearly. You are no longer fully inside the situation; you are observing it.

That changes your role in the exchange. Instead of reacting as a participant caught in the momentum of the situation, you begin evaluating what is happening before deciding how to continue.

That doesn't mean disengaging completely. It means you take a moment to understand what you are engaging with before proceeding. That moment can help you avoid automatic responses and deepen your understanding.

Small details that were easy to overlook at a faster pace become more noticeable. Urgency may feel less justified when considered carefully, and the request may not align as well with what you know once you take the time to think about it.

Even when nothing immediately stands out as wrong, slowing down creates a more stable foundation for whatever comes next.

Stability is important because it allows you to move forward with purpose instead of reaction. It ensures that each step you take is based on what you have considered, not just what has been presented to you.

This is what separates staying calm from simply waiting.

Waiting does not change the outcome. It is still possible to act under pressure after a delay if the underlying process has not changed. Staying calm is about changing the process itself. It is about returning to a state where you can think clearly.

When you are calm, you can look at situations without pressure or emotion influencing your perception. You can compare what you see or hear to what you know and identify inconsistencies more easily.

Verification becomes more reliable because, instead of rushing to confirm what you hope is true, you take the time to check information independently of what is presented to you.

Even disengaging becomes easier when you are calm. It is much harder to step away from something when you feel it needs to be handled immediately, but when you remove that pressure, creating distance becomes a more natural decision.

This is why staying calm is not just the first step; it is the step that makes all other steps possible.

If you've ever heard the phrase, "I should have known something was off," it's not because the information was hidden. The information was there. The time to process it was not.

Staying calm gives you access to the judgment you use in other parts of your life when decisions are not driven by urgency, emotion, misplaced trust, or reward.

Instead of moving at the speed of the situation, you return to one that supports clear thinking.

Over time, you recognize the feeling of being rushed sooner, become more comfortable pausing, and gain confidence in your ability to respond by setting your own pace.

Staying calm allows you to move through events at a pace that supports clear thinking, rather than being driven by urgency and emotion.

That is why this is the first step. Everything else depends on it.

Without it, the process is difficult to apply.

With it, the process becomes something you can rely on.

Evaluate

Once you create space by staying calm and pausing, the urgency and pressure to react begin to fade. You become more deliberate and focused, and that is where evaluation begins.

Evaluation is something most people do naturally because it feels like a normal part of everyday thinking. You see something, consider it, and decide what to do, and that process happens constantly without much thought. The difference here is not whether evaluation happens, but how it happens.

Under normal circumstances, evaluation is broad. You consider context, compare information, and allow time for different possibilities to surface. You can look at everything from multiple angles before deciding how to proceed.

When something feels urgent or familiar, the evaluation process can narrow. Instead of looking at the full picture, you focus on the part that feels most immediate. You look for information that supports what is being presented, rather than questioning whether the presentation itself makes sense.

This is not intentional on your part. It is a normal response to pressure.

When you believe something needs to be handled quickly, you adjust to match that pace. You look for the fastest way to understand and move forward, often relying on the information that is easiest to access.

The problem is that this information is presented in a way that guides your thinking toward a specific conclusion. When you evaluate only within that frame, you are not testing the information provided. You are confirming what has been suggested.

That is where evaluation needs to change. Instead of accepting the information as presented, you need to question the presentation itself.

You need to ask if it still makes sense when considered more carefully. Does the timing align with what you expect? Does the request match how similar things are normally handled? Does anything feel slightly out of place?

These questions are not meant to create doubt without a reason. They are meant to expand your perception beyond what is immediately visible, and that expansion is what makes evaluation effective.

Evaluation provides a broader view, letting you see details that may not have been obvious at first and helping you identify inconsistencies before they influence your decisions.

Thinking back to the situations with the wife and the child discussed earlier. Evaluation is where a different path could have been taken. In the moment, everything felt reasonable. The environment was familiar, the request made sense, and the urgency created an apparent need for action. But familiarity does not mean it's safe.

Without evaluation, those elements worked together to guide a decision. With evaluation, something different could have happened: a question might have been asked, a detail might have stood out, or the information might have been viewed from a slightly different perspective.

Evaluation is not about finding a problem. It is about determining whether the information presented in the situation holds up under careful examination.

There will be times when everything checks out, and the situation is legitimate. Not everything that feels off requires action. Evaluation does not change the outcome. It simply confirms that moving forward makes sense.

Other times, evaluation will reveal something that does not align, such as a minor inconsistency, a detail that does not meet expectations, or a request that seems less reasonable when considered more carefully. These signals indicate that the situation may require further attention.

Recognizing these signals does not mean you immediately know what's wrong. It means you've identified a reason to continue the process.

That is the purpose of evaluation: not to provide all the answers, but to determine whether you need to keep asking questions.

In practice, this can be as simple as taking an extra moment to read something again and decide if it makes sense, or to compare it to what you know from similar experiences. It doesn't require special tools or advanced knowledge. It simply requires attention that is not influenced by urgency or familiarity.

That is why staying calm comes first.

With calmness, evaluation becomes more objective, allowing you to examine the current situation without being pulled in a specific direction.

This is where you begin to take control of the process. Instead of being guided by what is presented, you guide your own understanding. You are no longer reacting; you are examining.

Evaluation is not a one-time action; it continues throughout the process. As new information becomes available, you can reassess and adjust your understanding. This flexibility is what makes the method adaptable to any situation.

You are not locked into a single interpretation. You refine your understanding as you go, which is why evaluation is a critical step.

It ensures that your decisions are based on the most complete understanding available in the moment, rather than on first impressions. That difference can prevent events from progressing in unintended ways.

Once you begin to evaluate effectively, the next step becomes clearer. You move from considering whether something makes sense to confirming whether it is true, and that transition leads to verification. But before you can verify anything, you need to know what you are verifying.

By continuing to evaluate, you eventually gain clarity and define the questions that need to be answered. Without those questions, the next step has no direction. Developing questions is why the evaluation step matters.

It takes the space created by staying calm and turns it into understanding that guides everything that follows.

Evaluation is not just about what you see; it's also about what you expect to see. When something matches your expectations, it feels right. When it doesn't, it stands out. The challenge is that expectations can be influenced.

When things are presented in a way that aligns with what you already believe, it becomes easy to accept because familiarity reinforces your expectations. Your evaluation may not extend beyond that initial confirmation.

This is why evaluation requires a slight adjustment.

Instead of only asking if something looks correct, you begin to ask if it behaves the way it should. That difference may seem small, but it changes how you interpret what you are seeing.

For example, a message may look correct in terms of format, language, and appearance. It may even include details that match your expectations, allowing it to pass a surface-level evaluation. But behavior is different from appearance.

Behavior includes timing, context, and interaction. You determine if the timing makes sense, if the situation fits what you would normally expect at that moment, and if the way the request is made aligns with how similar requests are usually handled.

These questions expand evaluation beyond what is immediately visible, helping you notice inconsistencies that may not stand out at first.

This matters because many situations are designed to appear normal. They may look correct, sound appropriate, and align with expectations in ways that reduce the likelihood of being questioned.

When you slow down and evaluate beyond what is presented, the situation becomes easier to understand.

If something behaves differently than expected, that difference becomes a signal that the situation may require further attention.

The purpose of evaluation is not to prove or disprove the situation. It is to determine whether it holds up under closer examination.

This often requires slowing down just enough to consider what might otherwise be overlooked, such as rereading something, considering how it fits your current context, or comparing it to similar experiences.

These actions are simple, but effective. They create a more complete understanding of the current situation and reduce the likelihood of making decisions based on incomplete information.

This also changes how you respond. Instead of feeling the need to act immediately, you begin to see the situation as something you have time to understand before acting, which reduces pressure and gives you the chance to take the time you need to evaluate properly.

Over time, this becomes a habit. You begin to evaluate everything more consistently, regardless of how it is presented, and you develop a sense for when something aligns and when it does not.

As you continue through this process, the next step becomes more defined. Evaluation helps you identify what needs confirmation and highlights areas requiring additional information.

From there, you move into verification, which builds on evaluation by taking the questions you have identified and seeking answers from sources independent of the current situation itself.

But without evaluation, those questions do not exist. There is nothing to verify.

That is why this step is essential.

Verify Everything

Once you take the time to evaluate things properly, you are ready to move to the next logical step: verification.

At first, verification may seem like part of evaluation, as though you are just looking at the same information in a slightly different way. However, there is an important difference between the two.

Evaluation asks whether something makes sense. Verification asks whether it is true. That distinction is what separates perception from confirmation.

Not only is it possible for something to feel wrong but to be right, as discussed earlier; it is also possible for something to make sense when evaluated and still be wrong.

Things can appear reasonable, align with expectations, and pass an initial evaluation, yet still be based on incomplete or misleading information. This is why verification is necessary: it moves you beyond what is presented and to what can be independently confirmed, regardless of the information you were first given.

Take, for example, the grandfather who approached me in a store while I was looking at printers. He asked if I could help him find a specific model he had seen advertised, one that could print an extreme number of pages from a single ink cartridge.

He had received the advertisement in the usual weekly sales flyer that arrived by mail, which made it feel trustworthy to him.

After spending some time talking with him, I realized he didn't need the advertised printer. What he really needed was something simple and reliable to print homework assignments and coloring book pages for his grandchildren, since their parents could not afford a printer.

As we continued talking, it became clear that the advertisement had shaped his understanding of what mattered most. He believed the large page count was the key factor, since the ad repeatedly emphasized it. Unfortunately, the number of pages was based on ideal testing conditions and did not reflect how the printer would perform in everyday use.

The advertisement was not false, but it did not give the full picture. It presented information in a way designed to influence a decision.

By the end of the conversation, the grandfather had bought a different printer and understood why it was the better choice for his needs.

He no longer felt like he was guessing. He understood what to expect from the printer, how it fit his needs, and why the original advertisement had not told the complete story.

What he really needed was not another advertisement or another sales pitch.

He needed independent verification.

Independence is the key to this step. Any information provided in the situation you are evaluating is influenced by its presentation. Even if it appears accurate, it remains connected to the same source that created the initial impression.

Verification requires you to step outside the original source of information and seek confirmation from sources not controlled by the situation you are evaluating.

This may seem like a small thing, but it changes your entire process. Instead of relying on what is given to you, you begin to seek information on your own, moving from receiving to confirming. That change gives you control over how the information is validated.

In everyday life, when something is important, you often look for a second source of information, check details, confirm facts, or ask someone else for input. These actions are not unusual; they are part of how people make informed decisions.

The challenge in situations like these is that the need for verification is not always obvious. Because the situation feels familiar or urgent, it may seem unnecessary to look beyond what is already available. The information provided appears sufficient, and the pressure to act quickly reduces the likelihood of seeking additional confirmation.

This is where the process can break down. If the evaluation has identified that something may not fully align, but verification is not applied, decisions are still based on incomplete information. The initial understanding remains unchallenged, and the situation continues.

The verification step interrupts the progression of events by introducing a step in which information is proven or confirmed outside of its original context. This often reveals differences between what is shared and what is independently validated.

These differences are what verification is designed to uncover. It is not about assuming something is wrong. It is about ensuring that what you are seeing can be supported beyond the immediate interaction.

In practice, this step can take many forms. It might involve contacting an organization directly, searching independently for accurate information, or verifying details with trusted sources rather than relying solely on what appears in front of you.

Verification does not need to be complicated. Often, just a brief check, a quick comparison, or a simple question can reveal whether information holds up under verification. If it does, you can move forward with greater confidence. If not, you have identified a reason to pause and reconsider.

Verification helps replace assumptions with evidence supported by multiple sources or perspectives. It does not require specialized knowledge. It simply requires the willingness to pause, evaluate carefully, and confirm what is true before acting.

Together, these steps form a progression, each building on the one before it, moving from recognition to understanding to confirmation, keeping you in control.

Without verification, decisions are made based on what is most immediate. With it, decisions are based on what has been examined and confirmed. That difference is what prevents some situations from advancing further. Once information is independently verified, it either supports or challenges what was presented; you are no longer relying solely on the original information. You are relying on what you have confirmed, and that is what gives this step its strength.

Once you begin to apply verification regularly, it becomes a natural extension of evaluation. You no longer stop at understanding; you continue testing what is presented. That is what ensures your decisions are grounded in truth, not just in the appearance of truth.

The more you apply verification, the clearer it becomes that not all sources of information carry the same weight. The information that is easiest to access is often the least reliable because it is presented in a way that supports the current situation, often without offering a complete view.

Verification changes that by expanding where you look. Instead of accepting information as complete, you begin to consider its source and how it can be independently verified, introducing an important distinction between convenience and reliability.

Convenience makes it easy to move forward. Verification helps ensure that moving forward is the right decision.

When something feels urgent, convenience often takes priority. Verification requires pausing to consider whether the information is sufficient. That pause is often where better decisions are made.

In practice, this means being intentional about how you confirm information. It may involve contacting an organization using trusted information you already have or accessing known sources directly rather than following links provided in the moment.

These actions may take a little more effort, but they often reveal inconsistencies that are easy to miss when relying on a single source or perspective.

Verification is also not limited to external sources. It can involve reviewing what you already know, comparing the situation to past experiences, and noticing details that do not align with how similar situations typically work.

These questions allow you to use your own knowledge during the verification process, adding an extra layer of confirmation to support what you find externally.

As you combine approaches, verification becomes more robust. You are not relying on a single method; you are building a clearer picture by using multiple reference points, which allows you to make decisions with confidence.

No matter how a situation is presented to you, the process remains the same. You seek confirmation outside the immediate context, compare information across different sources, and use what you know to support what you find. That consistency is what makes the process effective.

Over time, this will become a natural habit. You will begin to verify information automatically, without reminders, and the process will become part of how you engage with information instead of an extra step.

This habitual application ensures that verification is applied consistently, reduces the likelihood of acting on incomplete information, and improves decision-making.

Once you have verified what you can, the next step becomes clearer. You move from confirmation to action, deciding how to respond based on what you now understand. In some cases, that response may involve continuing with the situation now that it has been confirmed. In others, it may involve creating distance.

This is the point at which the next step in the process becomes real: disengaging.

Before you start that step, it is important to recognize what verification has accomplished. It has taken a situation based on presentation and emotion and turned it into one grounded in confirmation and confidence, replacing assumptions with evidence and providing the clarity needed to decide what to do next.

That is the purpose of this step: to ensure that what you act on is grounded in truth, and to give you the confidence to move forward based on that understanding.

With verification in place, the next step is a matter of choosing how to engage now that you understand the situation more clearly.

Calmly Disengage

Once you have taken the time to stay calm, evaluate, and verify what you can, you will reach a point where you need to make a decision. That decision is not always about what is true or false, but it is always about what you are going to do next. This is where disengagement begins.

It's important to note that disengagement is not avoidance. It is not stepping away from something that still needs to be resolved. Avoiding things in life can create problems by leaving matters unfinished or preventing solutions from being reached, but that is not what this step is about.

This step is about choosing not to continue an interaction that is influencing your thinking in a way that reduces your control.

The challenge is that by the time you reach this point, the interaction may already feel established. You may have already responded, asked questions, or taken steps that make it feel like you should continue, and there can be a sense of obligation, even if it is not clearly defined. That sense of obligation is part of what makes disengagement difficult.

When someone presents something in a way that feels legitimate, it creates an expectation of response. You often feel you should follow through, especially if the interaction seems connected to something important.

This is reinforced by the way many interactions are structured. They tend to begin with something that feels reasonable, such as a request for information, an offer of help, or an event that seems to require attention. As the interaction continues, it becomes more specific, more focused, and sometimes more urgent. Each step builds on the previous one, creating a sense of progression that makes it harder to step away, because doing so feels like interrupting something that has already started.

This is where disengagement becomes a decision rather than a reaction. You are not stepping away because anything has been resolved. You are stepping away because you have decided that continuing the interaction is not in your best interest and that decision is based on the process you have followed.

You created space by staying calm. You took time to evaluate the situation so you could understand what was being presented. Then you verified as much as you could to confirm its alignment with what was understood.

Sometimes the answer will be to continue. If everything aligns and has been confirmed as legitimate, there is no reason to disengage; the process has supported the decision to move forward.

But when something does not align, and often it will not, or when there is still uncertainty that cannot be resolved within the interaction itself, disengaging becomes the next step.

This step, like the others before, is not about certainty. You do not need to prove that something is wrong to disengage. You only need to recognize that continuing the interaction does not improve your understanding or control.

Disengaging can be simple. It might mean ending a call, closing a message, not responding further, or removing yourself from the immediate interaction. These actions may seem small, but they have a significant impact because they break the connection between you and the source of the influence.

This is what makes disengaging powerful. It finalizes the shift of control back to you. Instead of responding within the structure of the interaction, you create space to think and decide on your own terms. You are no longer limited to what is being presented in real time.

This is particularly important when the interaction involves urgency or emotion. As long as you remain engaged, those elements continue to influence your thinking and shape your response in ways you may not want them to.

That is why disengaging can be more effective than trying to manage the interaction while it's still happening. While you remain inside the situation, the factors shaping it continue to influence you. Disengaging creates space for clearer decisions.

There is also an emotional component to disengagement. It can feel uncomfortable to end an interaction without reaching a clear resolution. You may worry about being wrong, missing something important, or not responding in ways that feel appropriate, but these concerns are natural. They reflect how people are taught to interact. Continuing engagement often seems responsible, but in these situations, that assumption is not always true.

Because you have taken the time to stay calm, evaluate, and verify, you are not disengaging without reason. You are making an informed decision based on what you have observed, and that makes the action more confident. It is not avoidance. It is control.

The more you recognize when an interaction is not providing clarity, the more comfortable you become with stepping away. Hesitation decreases, and the decision becomes straightforward. Disengaging begins to feel less like an interruption and more like a natural part of protecting clear thinking.

As you become more comfortable with disengaging, another realization takes shape: disengaging is not the end of the process. Disengaging is when the process becomes more effective.

While you are engaged in an interaction, your attention is divided between understanding and responding in real time. Those two things together make clear thinking difficult, especially under pressure.

When you disengage, you no longer need to think or respond in real time. This allows you to focus entirely on understanding and deciding what to do next.

Instead of reacting within the structure that has been presented to you, you now operate within a structure that you control. This allows you to take the time you need to evaluate further, verify additional details, or seek input from other sources. This is where the early steps in the process can be applied more effectively.

Your evaluations become more thorough because you are not limited by time or other pressures. Verification becomes more reliable because you can access information without being guided by the original interaction. And your ability to recognize patterns improves because you are no longer focused on immediate responses.

This is why disengaging should not be viewed as a loss of progress. Instead of moving forward within the interaction, you move forward independently. That independence allows the process to continue without interference.

It is important to recognize that disengaging does not prevent you from returning to a situation if it proves to be legitimate.

If, after further evaluation and verification, everything aligns, you can engage again with greater confidence. Disengaging is not closing the door; it's creating the conditions needed to understand fully before continuing.

This perspective helps address a common concern about disengaging. Many fear that stepping away will lead to negative consequences or cause them to miss something important. That fear comes from the assumption that everything requires immediate attention.

When you remove that assumption, the decision to disengage becomes easier. Real events that require attention do not depend on immediate, unverified responses; they can withstand a pause, be revisited, and be confirmed independently.

This is what allows you to step away without concern. You are not abandoning the situation. You are choosing to handle it in a way that supports clear thinking.

This is particularly important in situations where the interaction itself is the primary source of pressure. As long as you remain engaged, that pressure continues to influence your decisions. By disengaging, you remove that influence and give yourself the ability to process information without the same level of external input. This is where clarity improves.

Once you step away, things often look different. Details that were not obvious before will become clear, the sense of urgency will feel less justified, and the overall structure of the situation will become easier to understand.

These changes are not the result of new information; they are the result of gaining a different perspective. A perspective that allows better decisions and reinforces the value of the process.

Each step we take builds on the previous one, and disengaging is the point at which progression becomes more independent. It allows you to continue the process without being influenced by the environment in which the situation was presented.

Over time, disengaging becomes more intuitive and easier. You will begin to recognize when interacting is no longer providing value and become comfortable stepping away. The decision becomes less about the specific situation and more about whether continuing supports clear thinking.

That is the key question: Does continuing improve your understanding, or does it bring more pressure?

If it introduces more pressure, disengaging is the appropriate response.

This is where the method's strength becomes clear. It does not rely on identifying specific problems. It relies on applying a consistent approach when things feel off. Disengaging is a critical part of that approach because it ensures you are not forced to make decisions in an environment that influences your thinking.

Once you reach this point, the next steps become more effective because they are applied without immediate pressure. That is what makes disengaging more than just stepping away. It is a transition from reacting within a situation to responding on your own terms.

In some situations, disengaging creates enough distance to begin the process again from a clearer perspective.

Information that once felt urgent may no longer carry the same pressure, and details that were difficult to recognize earlier may become easier to understand.

Returning to the beginning of the process is not failure. It is choosing to reassess the situation with greater clarity and control before deciding how to move forward.

Protect What Matters

Once you disengage from a situation, something important changes. The pressure is gone. You are no longer being asked to respond immediately or influenced by the pace or direction of the interaction. You have space to think clearly again, and that is where protection begins.

After disengaging, the goal becomes understanding whether anything needs attention. That understanding comes from a review. You take a moment to consider what happened, what actions were taken, and what information may have been involved.

Do not rush this part. It is simply a way to understand your position clearly before deciding what to do next.

Sometimes the review confirms that nothing further needs to be done. You recognized the event, followed the process, and disengaged before any meaningful interaction occurred. In those moments, the earlier steps worked exactly as intended.

The interaction ended before it gained control over your decisions, and you do not need to do anything else. That outcome matters because it reinforces the value of the process itself. You did not avoid a problem; through luck, you avoided it because you slowed down, thought clearly, and chose not to keep moving at the pace the situation was creating.

You may realize that some level of interaction has already taken place. Information may have been shared. A link may have been opened. An account may have been accessed. A payment attempt may have been made. These situations do not automatically mean that something is wrong, but they do indicate that it is worth taking a closer look.

This is where protection becomes practical.

Protection is not limited to one thing. It involves many areas, such as personal accounts, device access, personal information, financial access, conversations, or even confidence in your own decision-making. These areas are often connected to everyday life, which makes it important to understand what may have been exposed, what may have changed, and what may require attention.

For many people, protection immediately brings thoughts of passwords, banking information, or financial loss. Those things certainly matter, but protection is broader than that. It includes the systems and information that support everyday life.

This can involve email accounts connected to other services, devices containing personal conversations and photographs, social media accounts shared with family and friends, or financial systems connected to purchases, bills, and daily responsibilities. When one area is affected, the impact can extend beyond the original interaction itself.

That is why this step matters, even when the event appears small or takes very little time. Simple interactions can still involve information, account access, or systems connected to other parts of your life.

Taking a moment to review those connections creates awareness of what may require attention before problems have a chance to grow.

You may notice unfamiliar devices, messages, or transactions that do not belong or that were not there before.

These actions are not complicated, but they allow you to confirm that your current view of things still matches the reality that existed before the event.

If something doesn't look right, this step lets you address it early. So that you can hopefully avoid bigger issues later on.

That is the value of protection. Small problems are easier to manage before they become larger problems. A password can be changed before additional access occurs. A financial institution can be contacted before fraudulent activity begins. A suspicious device can be removed before more information is exposed.

These actions are not about panic; they are intended to reduce uncertainty and restore confidence in your understanding of the event.

This step also prevents urgency from continuing after the interaction ends. Many situations we discuss in the overall "Just Stay Calm" approach rely on creating pressure and pushing people to move quickly. Even after disengaging, it is easy to carry that urgency forward and feel like every action must happen immediately.

But protection is not about panic. It is about clarity.

You should take the time to understand your position, respond based on what you find, and avoid making decisions out of fear or pressure. That approach keeps the process steady and allows your actions to remain measured instead of reactive.

This matters because when people feel overwhelmed, they often rush toward what seems like an answer and react before fully understanding what has happened.

Slowing down allows you to separate what happened from what you fear may have happened. That difference matters because fear can shape decisions before clarity has a chance to form.

Over time, this way of thinking begins to extend beyond individual events. Protection becomes less about reacting to specific problems and more about maintaining awareness of what matters and how it is connected to your life.

You begin to think differently about access, information, and control. You become more aware of where important information is, how accounts interconnect, and which systems or devices have access to them. This does not require constant attention or technical expertise it simply requires awareness.

That awareness creates stability because it becomes easier to recognize when something does not align with your understanding of your environment. You know what belongs, what does not, and where to begin looking if something feels off. That understanding allows you to respond more effectively and with greater confidence.

This is what makes protection sustainable. It is not built on fear, but on constant vigilance, awareness, and consistency. You are not reacting to every possible problem. You are maintaining a position that supports better outcomes when events occur.

This involves simple habits practiced consistently over time. Like knowing how to access important accounts without relying on links inside messages. Understanding what devices connect to sensitive information. Knowing where important records are stored and paying attention to unexpected account notifications or password reset requests.

These actions may appear small on their own, but together they create a stronger understanding of your overall environment.

That understanding matters because not every situation feels wrong immediately. Some interactions only become questionable later, and maintaining awareness of your environment makes those inconsistencies easier to recognize.

It also supports recovery if something eventually goes wrong. No process removes every possible risk, and no person responds perfectly every time. What matters is how to respond once you recognize that something requires attention.

When accounts, systems, and information are organized and understood, it becomes easier to determine where to begin and which actions to take first. This reduces the stress that often appears when people feel overwhelmed.

Instead of reacting without understanding, you navigate information calmly and one step at a time. You know what information matters, where it connects, and what requires review. That clarity does not eliminate all problems, but it makes potential problems more manageable.

Protection is not just about preventing loss. It is about maintaining control over the things that matter to you and making sure that decisions made under pressure do not affect you afterward. It is also about preserving confidence in your ability to respond.

The goal is to feel capable of navigating technology with greater awareness and understanding. When people feel confident with technology, things naturally slow down, and they can more easily protect what matters; urgency loses much of its power.

The process becomes less about reacting to isolated events and more about maintaining an environment that supports clarity and stability.

Once a foundation of protection is in place, the process can continue. Not just to handle one-time situations, but to build confidence and awareness over time.

Because control is not temporary, it becomes part of how you manage what matters over time.

And when situations do require further action, that awareness and stability allow you to respond more clearly, more confidently, and with a better understanding of what needs to happen next.

Report When Needed

By this point, you have slowed down, taken the time to evaluate what you were seeing, and verified what you could check independent of the situation.

You have decided whether to continue engaging, and you have taken steps to protect your position.

You are now in control of how you respond, and that is what makes this next step different from how most people think about it.

Reporting is often associated with authority, escalation, or consequences. It can feel formal, uncomfortable, or even unnecessary, especially if no direct harm occurred. Many people assume that reporting is only required when something has gone wrong.

The truth is that reporting serves a different purpose.

It is not just about what happened to you. It is about what might happen to someone else.

This is an important shift in perspective because, up to this point, the process has focused on your ability to recognize, understand, and respond to situations in ways that maintain control. Reporting extends that process beyond your own experience and allows you to contribute to a broader awareness.

This means that when something is identified as misleading, deceptive, or potentially harmful, there is value in making that information available so others can benefit.

This step is not about obligation. It is about recognizing when what you experienced may help someone else.

You decide whether what you encountered is something that should be shared in a way that helps others recognize it more easily or not. In some cases, the answer will be no because the event may have been unclear, incomplete, or resolved without requiring further action. Even then, the process still worked because you maintained control.

In other cases, the answer may be yes because you recognize that what you encountered follows a pattern that could affect others. The way it was presented, how it influenced thinking, or how it attempted to create urgency or trust may be worth documenting. That is where reporting becomes useful.

Reporting creates a record not just for you, but for systems, organizations, or communities that track and respond to these patterns. This is not about creating a burden; it is about contributing to a larger picture.

Many of the protections that exist today are based on patterns identified over time. Those patterns are not discovered in isolation; they are built from repeated observations, shared experiences, and reported interactions. When you report something, you are adding to that understanding.

You are helping define what these situations look like, how they behave, and how they can be recognized. That may seem small in the moment, but it has lasting value because it allows systems to improve and communities to be informed, increasing the likelihood that similar events will be identified earlier in the future.

This is why reporting should not be viewed as separate from the process. It is a potential continuation of it, taking what you have already done and extending its impact.

Reporting does not require certainty. You do not need to prove that something is wrong. Recognizing that it may be wrong is enough to justify sharing information in a way that allows others to evaluate it.

This removes a common barrier many people face: hesitation to report because they are not completely sure what they encountered. Many people feel that without clear proof, reporting is of no help, but uncertainty is often part of the process. And it is precisely that uncertainty that needs to be shared.

Reporting allows uncertainty to be examined in a broader context, enabling patterns to emerge over time, even when individual situations are not fully defined.

Reporting can involve many forms: using a built-in reporting feature, contacting an organization directly, or sharing information within a trusted community. That flexibility ensures the step can be applied in different contexts without becoming difficult or time-consuming.

The goal is to ensure that what you observed is not lost, because it has value and is part of a pattern. That pattern can allow others to recognize and respond more effectively.

This is where the process begins to become part of a shared awareness, and that awareness strengthens into an overall system. Because while everyone is responsible for their own response, the ability to recognize and understand situations improves when information is shared.

The real role of reporting is not to assign blame or list consequences. It is to contribute to an understanding that helps others stay in control when they encounter similar situations.

As you become more comfortable with the idea of reporting, it stops feeling formal and starts feeling practical. Hesitation in reporting often stems from uncertainty about whether it is necessary, worth the effort, or will make a difference. These concerns are understandable, especially when the outcome is not immediately visible.

Looking at it slightly differently, reporting contributes to a larger process operating in the background. Even though individual reports may seem small, when combined, they create patterns that can be recognized and addressed. Systems improve, filters are adjusted, awareness increases, and that is how progress is made, not through a single action, but through consistent contributions over time.

Understanding this hopefully changes how you view this step: it is not about immediate results. It is about participation in a process that benefits others, even if the outcome is not directly visible to you. You are not responsible for solving the problem. You are simply contributing to understanding the problem and to the future protection of all.

For this to work as designed, reporting doesn't need to include every detail or provide a complete analysis. It simply needs to capture what you observed in a way that makes sense. Even partial information has value.

If reporting feels complicated, it becomes less likely to happen. If it feels accessible, it becomes part of the process. That is the balance this step is designed to maintain.

Reporting should be available when needed, but not overwhelming; useful, but not a burden. It is also important to note that reporting is not limited to formal channels. While formal reporting is appropriate at times, sharing information within a trusted group can have value too.

A conversation with a friend, a discussion with family members, or a note to a colleague all contribute to awareness in different ways. But they all help others understand what to look for and reinforce that these situations are not isolated to just one person.

This connection between reporting and sharing is important because it shows that the process does not end with individual action. It extends to how information moves between people, and that movement strengthens awareness over time.

It also sets up the final step in this process. Once something has been recognized, evaluated, verified, and, when appropriate, reported, there is an opportunity to take it one step further.

Ensure the knowledge gained is not lost and becomes part of how others think and respond moving forward.

Before moving into the next step, let's review what reporting accomplishes. It takes individual experiences and connects them to a broader awareness, allowing what you encountered to help others recognize similar situations.

That is what makes this step important. It extends the value of what you have already done beyond your own experience, allowing the opportunity to take the process one step further.

Share With Others

Learning to notice moments that might have passed unnoticed before is no small matter.

That awareness has value beyond any single situation, and that is where this final step begins.

Sharing what you have learned can feel more complicated than it really is. Something complex that requires a technical background. But sharing is simpler than that. It's the passing on of awareness.

Not in a way that creates fear, and not in a way that overwhelms others, but in a way that helps them recognize what you've learned to see.

This step isn't about retelling every detail of your experience. It's about communicating the same patterns you've noticed throughout this process. The feeling of urgency, the sense of familiarity, the appearance of value, the shift in thinking, and the need to pause.

These patterns aren't tied to a single situation. They repeat constantly. They show up in different forms but follow the same structure, making the act of sharing far more effective. You're not trying to prepare someone for specific scenarios; you're helping them recognize a pattern that can appear anywhere.

This aligns with an idea introduced earlier: these situations are rarely built around specific people. They are built around patterns that reach many people at once, waiting for moments when someone is distracted, overwhelmed, rushed, or simply trying to do the right thing.

That is part of why sharing matters.

When people hear how these situations unfold, they begin to recognize the patterns more clearly in their own lives. Not because they memorized a specific example, but because they understand the feeling of being rushed, the appearance of familiarity, or the pressure to act before fully thinking things through.

Sharing gives people a reference point. Something to recognize when a moment feels off. A way to pause and think, "I have seen something like this before. I do not need to rush."

That is what allows awareness to extend beyond your own experience.

What you have learned can help others think more clearly without requiring formal training or expertise. Sometimes a simple conversation, example, or explanation is enough to help someone recognize a situation differently.

These conversations do not need to be perfect or highly structured. They only need to help people understand that when something feels rushed, emotional, or slightly off, there is value in slowing down before responding.

The tone of those sharing matters.

If the goal becomes fear, shame, or embarrassment, people often stop listening and begin to feel overwhelmed, ashamed, or targeted. But when the goal is awareness and calm understanding, people become more confident in their ability to respond when situations feel wrong.

So, the approach remains the same: calm, clear, and confident.

The goal is not to frighten people or make them feel embarrassed about missing something. It is to help them understand how situations like these work and why slowing down matters.

When people feel overwhelmed or ashamed, they often stop listening. But when conversations are grounded in calm awareness and understanding, people become more open to recognizing patterns and responding differently in the future.

Sharing also reinforces your own understanding.

Explaining something to another person often helps clarify it within yourself. You begin to recognize the patterns more consistently, and the process becomes more natural because you have taken the time to put it into words.

Over time, these conversations create broader awareness. People begin to recognize situations earlier, respond more calmly, and share what they have learned with others. That is how awareness grows beyond a single experience and begins helping entire communities think more clearly.

It evolves naturally, not through formal instruction, but through simple conversations and repeated interactions. Each time the idea is shared, it has the potential to help someone else pause, think more clearly, and recognize when something feels off.

That is what allows awareness to move beyond a single situation or experience.

What you learn does not help you alone. It creates opportunities to help other people move through difficult moments more calmly and with greater confidence. That is what sharing makes possible.

As sharing becomes part of how you think and communicate, it takes on a different role. It is no longer something you do only after an experience. It becomes something you carry with you.

You notice opportunities to share in everyday conversations, not in a way that feels forced or overly structured, but in a way that naturally helps people think differently about situations and experiences.

These moments happen naturally. Someone mentions a message that felt unusual, an unexpected call, or a situation where they felt pressured, and those become opportunities to share what you have learned.

You don't need to explain everything or walk through every step. You only need to introduce the idea that there is a way to respond, using simple reminders like "Just stay calm," "Take a second look," "Make sure you check things another way." Small statements like these can naturally support the process. They are not instructions. They are cues, pointing back to everything you've learned. This is what makes the process scalable.

It does not require full explanations every time. It allows the core ideas to be communicated in a way that's easy to remember and apply. Over time, these cues begin to connect with experiences, and people start to recognize when something feels urgent, familiar, emotional, or too good to be true. They associate those feelings with the need to pause and think, and that is how awareness spreads.

Not through complexity, but through repetition and clarity.

This is where the idea of teaching becomes more defined.

Teaching doesn't require formal settings or structured lessons. It happens through conversation, through examples, and through shared understanding. It's about helping others see what you've learned to recognize.

That role doesn't require expertise. It requires experience, awareness, and the ability to communicate clearly.

In real conversations, the roles of learning and guiding aren't fixed roles. Sometimes you are the one experiencing a situation, trying to understand it. Other times, you are helping someone else slow down, think clearly, and recognize what's happening. In both cases, the process is the same: stay calm, create space to think, and help others do the same.

It is not one person teaching while another learns. It's a continuous exchange of awareness with people contributing from their own experiences and everyone benefiting from what is shared.

This is how the process becomes part of a community, not through formal adoption, but through repeated use.

As more people recognize the patterns and apply the steps, the overall environment shifts. Situations that rely on urgency become less effective when people pause. Events that rely on familiarity become less convincing when people evaluate. Moments that rely on incomplete information become less successful when people verify.

This collective response gradually reduces the effectiveness of those situations, creating a shift away from reacting to awareness, from individual control to shared understanding.

This is the larger impact of the "Just Stay Calm" process.

It's not just about handling individual situations. It's about changing how those situations are experienced across a wider group, and that change doesn't happen all at once.

It happens gradually, through repeated sharing and application. Each conversation contributes. Each example reinforces the idea. Each person who applies the process adds to the overall awareness.

This is why the final step is not an ending. It's a continuation.

It ensures the process doesn't stop with a single person or experience. It grows, adapts, and reaches others in ways that are not always visible, but remain consistently impactful.

And as it spreads, it becomes something more than a method.

It becomes a mindset, a way of approaching everything through calmness, clarity, and control.

That is what you carry forward.

Not just the steps, but the thinking behind them.

Because once you see these patterns, you cannot unsee them. Once you understand how to respond, you naturally want others to have that same ability.

That is the final evolution.

To take what you've learned and allow it to move beyond you to make it part of how others think, respond, and stay in control, and in doing so, to contribute to something that continues long after any single event has passed.

Now That You See It

By now, something has probably changed for you. Not in the situations themselves, but in how you experience them.

The messages, calls, offers, and requests will still happen. They will still feel familiar, urgent, emotional, or valuable. They will still appear at moments when your attention is divided or your time feels limited. That hasn't changed. What has changed is what happens next.

Where there was once a quick reaction, there is now a pause. Where there was a sense of urgency, there is now awareness of that urgency. Where there was once a decision made within the moment, there is now a decision made about the moment. That shift is the purpose of this entire process.

It's not about avoiding anything. It's about recognizing what is happening in real time and responding in a way that keeps you in control.

This is where the process becomes practical, not as a set of steps to remember, but as something that happens naturally once you have seen it enough times. To understand how this works, let's walk through a few simple everyday moments.

A message appears. It looks familiar. The name is recognizable, the format is expected, and the request seems reasonable. It asks for something small, something that would normally require much thought. Before, this situation would have moved quickly. You would have read it, accepted it, and responded. **See images A1 and A2 in Appendix A.**

Now, something different happens. There's a pause not because you're unsure, but because you recognize the pattern. That sense of familiarity is enough to slow you down. In that pause, you begin to evaluate.

Does this make sense? Does the timing align with what you know? Is anything about this not meeting your expectations? You might not have answers yet, but you've identified a reason to look deeper.

From here, you verify the information independently. You check beyond the message itself to confirm whether the request is real. If it is, you move forward with confidence. If it's not, the situation ends there without escalation, confusion, or unnecessary impact.

Here's a slightly different moment.

A call comes in; the voice is calm, the explanation is clear, and the situation feels important. There's a sense that something needs to be handled now and that waiting could cause a problem. Before, urgency would have guided your response; you may have focused on resolving the issue as quickly as possible. **See images B1 and B2 in Appendix A.**

Now, the urgency stands out, but it doesn't control you. Recognizing it creates space. In that space, you evaluate again. Does this process align with how similar situations are usually handled? Is the request consistent with what you know? Can I confirm this independently? You move through the same process: stay calm, evaluate, verify, and disengage if needed.

Each step flows to the next not because you're forcing it, but because you understand the structure. That understanding changes everything. You no longer respond to the situation as it is presented. You respond to the patterns within it. And that is what allows you to stay in control.

This is not about perfection. There will still be unclear moments, decisions that take time, or additional steps needed. But now, you have a way to move through those moments. You are no longer relying on instinct alone; you have a clear, calm, structured way to move through each moment.

You are applying a process that supports clear thinking, a process that is simple at its core.

It begins with staying calm. Improves by evaluating. Becomes clear through verification. And it allows you to disengage when needed. It ensures you protect your position. Then it enables you to report and share when appropriate and helpful. Each step supports the others and reinforces the idea that you don't need to react immediately to respond effectively.

That is the essence of what has changed. You have moved from reacting to responding, from following to controlling, and from hoping to knowing. That shift determines the outcome of these situations. Once you respond intentionally, the situation's structure no longer dictates your decisions. You do.

That is where control exists.

Once you recognize it, it becomes something you can rely on not just in a single moment, but in any moment when something feels off.

That is what it means to "see it."

Not just to understand it, but to recognize it as it happens. Once you can do that, the process becomes something you carry with you, not something you have to recall. It becomes part of how you think, allowing everything you've learned to continue naturally over time.

As you carry this awareness forward, another realization should have happened.

Nothing in this process is new. Every step you've worked through here is something you were already capable of doing. You could already pause to question what's being presented, use critical thinking to confirm information, step away when needed, and protect what matters to you.

What was missing wasn't the ability. It was structure. A way to bring those abilities together in the moments where they are most needed. That's what this process gives you. It doesn't give you something you didn't already have. It gives you a way to use what you already have more effectively. And that is why it works.

It isn't built on complexity. It's built on recognizing how these situations are presented, how your thinking is influenced, and when to pause and take control.

Once that recognition is in place, everything else follows naturally. You don't need to force the process or remember every step in detail. You only need to notice the moments as they happen.

That is your entry point. From there, the process unfolds. You stay calm. You evaluate. You verify. You disengage if needed. You protect what matters. Then you report what you learned or observed. Finally, you share as appropriate.

All the steps exist together as a single method, but none of them work without that first moment of recognition. That is what you've gained: not just knowledge, but awareness.

Awareness that allows you to respond differently. Awareness that gives you control, even when others are designing ways to take control away. Awareness that helps you see things now that would have passed unnoticed before.

You will begin to recognize patterns faster, pause sooner, and ask a question before acting, thereby strengthening the process. You make it more natural. You turn it into something you can rely on.

That is the final goal. Not perfection. Progress.

Progress means the process continues to evolve.

This is where confidence comes from, not from knowing every possible scenario, but from knowing how to respond when a scenario presents itself. You don't need to predict what will happen. You only need to recognize it when it happens.

Once you recognize it, you have a way forward. You are no longer guessing or reacting. You are applying a process that supports clear thinking and allows you to navigate situations with confidence.

Not because situations are simple, but because your response is.

That is what makes this method so powerful.

It doesn't change who you are. It helps you remain who you are, even when pulled in a different direction. That is what you carry forward: not just a method, but a mindset.

A way of staying calm, grounded, aware, confident, and in control.

Once you have that, you won't lose it, because you have seen how it works, experienced the difference, and know that when the next moment comes, you will recognize it.

You will pause before you respond.

And you will…

Just Stay Calm.

Appendix A:

Demonstration of Situations

The examples in this appendix include both email and voicemail situations, presented in a compare-and-contrast format to highlight how small differences in presentation can influence decisions.

These examples are not meant to make you suspicious of everything you see or encounter online or in everyday life. Their purpose is to help you recognize how situations can appear familiar, trustworthy, urgent, or emotionally convincing, while still influencing the way you think and respond.

As you review the examples, pay attention not only to what is being presented, but also to how it is presented. Notice how urgency, familiarity, perceived value, pressure, or emotional connection can subtly influence decision-making in ways that are easy to overlook in the moment.

These examples are not here to create fear. They are here to help you recognize situations more clearly and respond more calmly.

Image A1 - Safer Communication Pattern

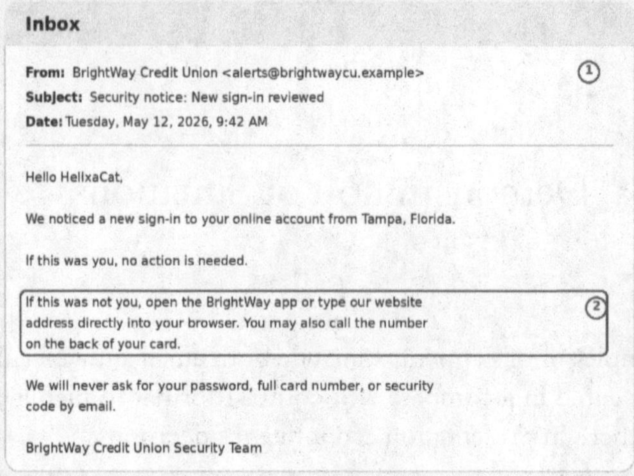
Inbox

From: BrightWay Credit Union <alerts@brightwaycu.example> ①

Subject: Security notice: New sign-in reviewed

Date: Tuesday, May 12, 2026, 9:42 AM

Hello HelixaCat,

We noticed a new sign-in to your online account from Tampa, Florida.

If this was you, no action is needed.

If this was not you, open the BrightWay app or type our website address directly into your browser. You may also call the number on the back of your card. ②

We will never ask for your password, full card number, or security code by email.

BrightWay Credit Union Security Team

Example A1: A safer message pattern with independent verification options

1. Recognizable Sender Information

The message appears to come from a legitimate domain associated with the organization. Notice that the domain includes the expected words and ends with a proper .com. This helps you recognize when a message is likely authentic.

2. Independent Verification

Instead of asking you to click a link, the message encourages verification through independent steps:

Open the official app.

Type the website manually.

Call the number listed on the back of the card.

This approach allows you to confirm the situation outside of the message itself.

The message also avoids creating immediate pressure. It explains the concern without demanding instant action, giving you the space to respond thoughtfully.

Image A2 - Pressure-Based Communication Pattern

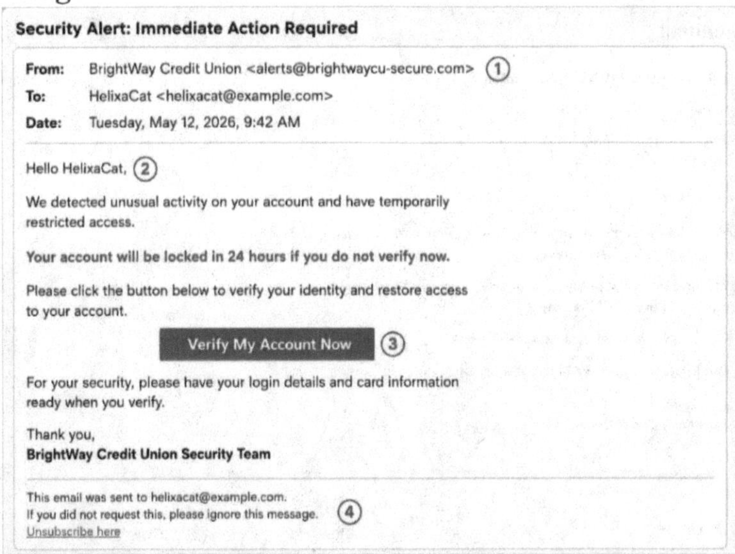
Security Alert: Immediate Action Required

From: BrightWay Credit Union <alerts@brightwaycu-secure.com> ①
To: HelixaCat <helixacat@example.com>
Date: Tuesday, May 12, 2026, 9:42 AM

Hello HelixaCat, ②

We detected unusual activity on your account and have temporarily restricted access.

Your account will be locked in 24 hours if you do not verify now.

Please click the button below to verify your identity and restore access to your account.

Verify My Account Now ③

For your security, please have your login details and card information ready when you verify.

Thank you,
BrightWay Credit Union Security Team

This email was sent to helixacat@example.com.
If you did not request this, please ignore this message. ④
Unsubscribe here

1. Slightly Different Sender Address

The sender's information appears similar to that of a legitimate source, but the domain doesn't match the expected format. Extra words and altered spelling are common tactics to imitate trusted organizations.

2. Urgency and Time Pressure

The message tries to create urgency by threatening account closure or other consequences within a short timeframe. This pressure is designed to make you act quickly, without pausing to evaluate.

3. Direct Verification Link

Instead of encouraging independent verification, the message keeps you inside it by providing an embedded link.

4. Requests for Sensitive Information

The message asks you to have login or card information ready. Legitimate organizations usually provide multiple ways to verify identity and do not pressure users to provide or share sensitive information through links inside unexpected messages.

Image B1 - Safer Communication Pattern

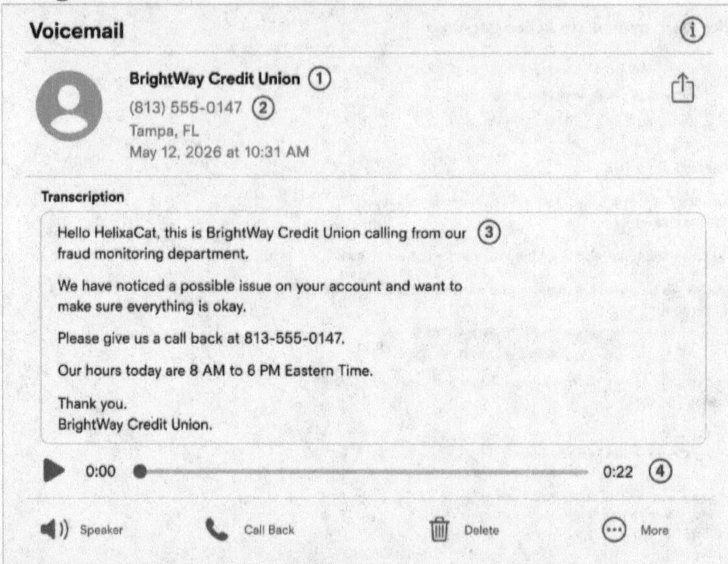

1. Clear Organization Identification

The voicemail clearly identifies the organization. This provides a reliable starting point for understanding who is contacting you.

2. Callback Through Known Contact Information

The message includes a phone number and lets the listener decide how and when to respond. This gives control over the interaction.

3. Calm and Non-Urgent Language

The voicemail explains that there may be an issue and asks the listener to return the call, without pressure or threats.

4. Time to Verify

The message allows space for independent verification before responding. The listener can pause, think clearly, and verify the call's legitimacy through trusted sources.

Image B2 - Pressure-Based Communication Pattern

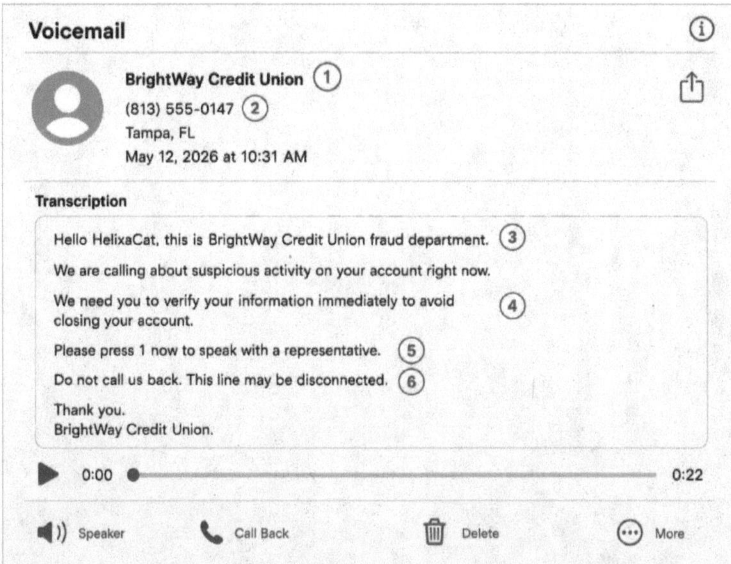

1. **Similar Appearance Does Not Guarantee Legitimacy**

The voicemail may appear professional and familiar. Scam calls can imitate the tone, structure, and language of legitimate organizations.

2. **Immediate Pressure**

The voicemail creates urgency, suggesting that action must happen immediately to avoid consequences.

3. **Forced Interaction**

The voicemail attempts to keep the listener engaged by directing them to press buttons or continue the interaction without pause.

4. **Discouraging Independent Verification**

Discouraging callbacks through known channels or preventing independent verification removes an important layer of protection.

Appendix B

Common Pressure Situations

Not every situation that feels unusual, rushed, or emotionally charged is harmful. Sometimes, there are perfectly reasonable explanations for why something initially feels off.

This appendix is designed to help you slow down and think through situations more calmly before reacting. The examples included here are not meant to provide perfect answers for every scenario. Instead, they demonstrate how taking a moment to evaluate things more carefully can often change how a situation is understood.

The goal is simple: create enough space to think clearly, ask questions, and avoid reacting solely from pressure, urgency, or emotion.

When something feels urgent, review how it is being presented. Real situations do not require immediate action without the ability to verify.

What pushes you to act fast?	Why is this not legitimate?	What to do instead.
"You will be arrested if you do not pay now."	Real legal actions do not demand immediate payment over the phone.	**Pause and verify through official channels.**
"Your grandchild needs money right now."	Real emergencies can be confirmed through family or direct contact.	**Call the family member directly.**
"Your power will be shut off immediately."	Utility companies provide notice and multiple ways to verify.	**Contact the provider using the information on your bill.**
"Your account is locked. Act now."	Legitimate services allow login verification through known channels.	**Log in directly through the official website.**
"You have a refund waiting, but it expires today."	Real refunds do not disappear instantly without notice.	**Check your account through official sources.**
"Suspicious activity detected, confirm immediately."	Security alerts allow time and multiple verification paths.	**Verify through your bank or service directly.**

"You won a prize, claim it now."	Legitimate winnings do not require immediate action or pressure.	**Pause and confirm legitimacy independently.**
"This offer is only available right now."	Real opportunities allow time to consider and verify.	**Take time before committing.**
"We need remote access to fix your issue now."	Legitimate support does not rush access without verification.	**Contact support through known channels.**
"Package delivery failed, update details now."	Delivery services provide consistent tracking methods.	**Check directly through the official carrier site.**
"Immediate payment required to avoid penalties."	Real billing processes include statements and time to respond.	**Review your account independently.**
"Act now to secure your job/payment."	Legitimate offers allow time to review terms.	**Verify the company and offer before responding.**

Very few real situations require immediate action without the ability to verify.

Final Reflection

If you've made it this far, it's worth pausing to recognize what has happened. You haven't just read through a set of ideas; you've followed a shift. A shift that moves us from reacting to responding, from urgency to awareness, and from uncertainty to control. That shift is exactly what this process was designed to create.

And that shift doesn't belong in the pages of this book only. It now belongs to you.

It belongs to you because these were not new concepts. You already had the ability to pause, to question, to confirm, to step away, to protect what matters, to report bad behavior, and to help others understand.

What you have now is the ability to bring all those things together calmly in the moments where they are needed most, and that is what makes this different.

You are not relying on memorization, nor are you trying to predict every possible scenario. You are recognizing patterns and responding with intention, and that is something you can apply in any situation.

Think back to the examples we discussed.

First, there was the wife searching for medical equipment her husband needed. She was not careless; she was solving a real problem during a stressful moment. The site felt familiar, helpful, and specific enough to trust. Later, the follow-up email seemed like a second chance to get it right. In both moments, the steps in this book of staying calm, evaluating, verifying independently, disengaging when necessary, and protecting accounts afterward would have created the space she needed to respond effectively.

Then the child in the online game who wasn't trying to do anything wrong. The interaction felt normal because it happened in a familiar environment, and the promise of leveling up created value. When a short time limit was added, urgency entered the scene. The card's protection prevented a financial mistake; that the steps in this book could have prevented earlier by teaching the child to pause, evaluate the request, verify with an adult, and disengage before acting.

And finally, the grandfather was trying to make the best decision he could with limited information. Nothing about the situation was malicious, but the way the information was presented could have led to a poor outcome for the grandfather. But by slowing down, evaluating the real need, and distinguishing between what was advertised and what was intended, the outcome improved.

None of these situations were identical, yet the response remained the same. The details changed, but the process did not. Each of these moments reflects the same idea.

Situations themselves don't need to be extreme to matter. This process applies to everyday decisions just as much as it does to high-risk situations. That is exactly why it works. It isn't designed for rare events; it's designed for events we encounter every day.

There will still be moments when things feel unclear and situations that take time to understand. There may even be times when you look back and realize you would respond differently now, and that is expected. It is part of learning to recognize these situations more clearly.

Each of those moments strengthens the process. They improve your ability to recognize what's happening and increase your ability to respond in ways that keep you in control. Over time, this becomes natural. You won't think about each step. You will simply notice the moment.

And in that moment, you will pause.

You will create space. And from that space, everything else becomes possible.

That is what you carry with you: not just a method, but a way of thinking. A way of staying grounded when someone or something tries to rush you. A way of thinking clearly when something tries to confuse you. A way to stay in control when something tries to take that control away.

Once you have that mindset, you will never lose it because once you have seen it, used it, and you understand how it works. It will never go away.

So, when the next challenging moment comes, you will recognize it.

You will slow down.

You will respond.

And that is the difference.

That is the value.

And that is what continues long after this book ends.

Trusted Verification Contacts

This page is for quick access when something feels urgent. Fill in the contacts you trust so you can verify information independently when needed.

Do not store passwords or sensitive account details here. This page is for contact information only.

Include banks, credit card providers, utilities, family members, and any services you rely on.

Name: ____________________ **Number:** ____________________

Email: ____________________ **Website:** ____________________

Name: ____________________ **Number:** ____________________

Email: ____________________ **Website:** ____________________

Name: ____________________ **Number:** ____________________

Email: ____________________ **Website:** ____________________

Name: ____________________ **Number:** ____________________

Email: ____________________ **Website:** ____________________

Name: ____________________ **Number:** ____________________

Email: ____________________ **Website:** ____________________

Name: ______________________ Number: ____________________

Email: _____________________ Website: ___________________

Name: ______________________ Number: ____________________

Email: _____________________ Website: ___________________

Name: ______________________ Number: ____________________

Email: _____________________ Website: ___________________

Name: ______________________ Number: ____________________

Email: _____________________ Website: ___________________

Name: ______________________ Number: ____________________

Email: _____________________ Website: ___________________

Name: ______________________ Number: ____________________

Email: _____________________ Website: ___________________

Trusted Verification Contacts

This page is for quick access when something feels urgent. Fill in the contacts you trust so you can verify information independently when needed.

Do not store passwords or sensitive account details here. This page is for contact information only.

Include banks, credit card providers, utilities, family members, and any services you rely on.

This page may be copied for personal use or shared with family members who may benefit from maintaining their own trusted verification contacts.

Name: ______________________ Number: ____________________

Email: _____________________ Website: ___________________

Name: ______________________ Number: ____________________

Email: _____________________ Website: ___________________

Name: ______________________ Number: ____________________

Email: _____________________ Website: ___________________

Name: ______________________ Number: ____________________

Email: _____________________ Website: ___________________

Name: ____________________ **Number:** ____________________

Email: ____________________ **Website:** ____________________

Name: ____________________ **Number:** ____________________

Email: ____________________ **Website:** ____________________

Name: ____________________ **Number:** ____________________

Email: ____________________ **Website:** ____________________

Name: ____________________ **Number:** ____________________

Email: ____________________ **Website:** ____________________

Name: ____________________ **Number:** ____________________

Email: ____________________ **Website:** ____________________

Name: ____________________ **Number:** ____________________

Email: ____________________ **Website:** ____________________

What, you're still here?

I thought you would have moved on by now.

Well, if you are still reading, there is one more.

You're going to have to turn the page.

This works in real-world, face-to-face encounters too.

Have you ever had someone knock on your door and start talking before you could even think?

Or approached at a gas station with a story that didn't sit right?

Maybe you've found yourself face-to-face with someone somewhere else, where something felt off, but you couldn't explain why?

Those moments feel different because there's no screen between you and the other person.

But they are not different. They follow the same patterns. They create the same pressure. And they rely on the same thing: your reaction.

Everything we've worked through in this book still applies in person.

1. Stay Calm even when someone is standing right in front of you, trying to control the pace of the moment.
2. Still evaluate what is being said, not just the words, but how they are delivered: the speed, urgency, emotion, and physical mannerisms.
3. Verify, even if that only means saying you need a moment and refusing to respond immediately after stepping away and grabbing a glass of water to create some space.
4. Disengage: step back, hold up your look away, end the conversation, walk away, or drive away without needing to explain why.
5. Protect what matters: your personal information, your time, your attention, or your physical space.
6. Report when appropriate, especially if the situation could affect others.
7. And share what you have learned so others are protected.

As you can see, the steps didn't change. The environment did.

The only thing that changes is the distance.

Without a screen, the pressure can feel stronger, the urgency more immediate. The expectation to respond can make it harder to step away.

That is exactly why the same approach matters even more.

You are not required to respond just because someone is present.

You are not required to continue just because a conversation has started.

You are allowed to pause.

You are allowed to step away.

You are allowed to decide what happens next.

Because the moment you stop reacting and start deciding, everything changes for the better.

Not for them.

For you.

And that is what this has always been about.

No one should feel like they must navigate situations like these alone.

Sometimes the most important thing is simply having a place where people can slow down, ask questions, and learn from each other without judgment.

That is part of why communities like Shade Tree IT are being built.

Not around fear or pretending to know everything, but around helping people think more clearly, feel more confident, and support one another through the situations, technology, and decisions life places in front of them.

So, whether it is a message, a call, an email, a website, or someone standing right in front of you, the process does not go away, because it can be carried with you anywhere.

So don't panic.

Just Stay Calm.

Just Stay Calm

For when something feels urgent, unusual, or just slightly off. Just follow the steps. Just Stay Calm.

1. Stay Calm
• Pause before responding.
• Give yourself space to think.

2. Always Evaluate
• Does this make sense?
• Does the timing feel right?
• Is anything slightly off?

3. Verify Everything
• Check outside the situation.
• Use sources you already trust.

4. Calmly Disengage
• You do not have to continue.
• Step away from pressure.
• Create space to think clearly.

5. Protect What Matters
• Review what was shared.
• Check accounts and access.
• Secure anything that needs attention.

6. Report If Needed
• Share what you encountered.
• Support broader awareness.

7. Share With Others
• Pass on awareness, not fear.
• Keep it simple and clear.
• Help others recognize the moment.

About the Author

Donald Tate has spent most of his life helping people feel safer, confident, and more capable in difficult situations. After high school, he served in the United States Army before beginning a long career in information technology, support, leadership, and training.

Throughout his career, Donald became known not just for solving technical issues but for teaching people how to avoid the same problems in the future through calm understanding, practical guidance, and confidence-building instruction. Within just a few years of entering the private sector, he was already training support staff and helping build teams focused on education as much as technology.

Over the years, Donald moved into senior leadership and executive roles while staying connected to the people and systems he supported. His approach has always been centered around the belief that people make better decisions when they understand what is happening, why it matters, and how they can respond calmly under pressure. This approach has evolved into the Just Stay Calm framework, helping people "just stay calm."

Donald is the founder of **HelixaLogic**, a technology support and education initiative focused on helping people better understand and navigate the digital world with greater confidence and clarity.

Today, the Just Stay Calm framework supports books, workshops, and community conversations to help people navigate technology and digital decision-making with greater confidence and clarity.

www.ingramcontent.com/pod-product-compliance
Lightning Source LLC
LaVergne TN
LVHW042057230926
848801LV00007B/155
* 9 7 9 8 9 9 6 4 2 3 3 0 9 *